WALKMAN

MICHAEL ROBBINS

WALKMAN

PENGUIN POETS

PENGUIN BOOKS
An imprint of Penguin Random House LLC
penguinrandomhouse.com

Page 65 constitutes an extension of this copyright page.

LIBRARY OF CONGRESS CATALOGING-IN-PUBLICATION DATA
Names: Robbins, Michael, 1972– author.
Title: Walkman / Michael Robbins.
Description: New York : Penguin Books, [2021] | Series: Penguin poets
Identifiers: LCCN 2020043412 (print) | LCCN 2020043413 (ebook) |
    ISBN 9780143134909 (paperback) | ISBN 9780525506577 (ebook)
Subjects: LCGFT: Poetry.
Classification: LCC PS3618.O315244 W35 2021 (print) | LCC PS3618.O315244 (ebook) |
    DDC 811/.6—dc23
LC record available at https://lccn.loc.gov/2020043412
LC ebook record available at https://lccn.loc.gov/2020043413

Printed in the United States of America
1st Printing

Set in Adobe Garamond Pro
Designed by Ginger Legato

CONTENTS

Walkman   1

The Deep Heart's Core   11

You Haven't Texted Since Saturday   12

Shed   17

When Didn't I Know It   19

What They Mean   22

CVS on Fire   23

Bear   25

Flare   26

Prayer   27

I'm Talking to Trucks   28

Throwing the *Yijing* in Bullhead City   31

Poem   33

County Fair   34

To Anthony Madrid   35

Past One O'Clock   36

The Park Is Full of People   41

In Time of Plague   43

John Says the Elders Came Over   46

The Seasons   48

Acknowledgments   65

At least there's pretty lights

—MEN AT WORK

WALKMAN

Walkman

I didn't mean to quit drinking,
it just sort of happened.
I'd always assumed
it'd be difficult, or not
difficult, exactly,
but impossible.
Then one New Year's Eve
twenty years ago
at the VFW, Craig and I
were drinking beer
from brown bottles,
peeling the labels off
into little confetti nests.
In Mexico
the previous New Year's Eve,
I'd started drinking
again after a year sober.
I traveled by myself
in Oaxaca for a month
and had at least two
beautiful experiences.
The bus I was on broke
down in the mountains
and I watched the stars blink
on with a Mexican girl
who later sent me a letter
I never answered. That's one
of the experiences. The others
are secrets. We left the VFW

at a reasonable hour for once.
I never took another drink.
I'm not sure why not.
I don't think it had anything
to do with me. I think
it was a miracle. Like when
the hero at the last
second pulls the lever to switch
the train to the track the heroine's
not tied to. I was always broke
in those days, whereas now I'm just
poor. I brought a Walkman
and a backpack stuffed with
cassettes to Oaxaca. I was sick
of them all within a week
and longed to buy a new tape
but couldn't spare the pesos.
I listened to *Live Through This*
at the Zapotec ruins
of Monte Albán,
Rumours on the bus to DF.
At Puerto Ángel,
my headphones leaking
tinny discord
across a rooftop bar,
I sat watching the ocean.
An American man about the age
I am now
asked me what I was listening to.

I said Sonic Youth. He asked
which album, I said *Sister*.
He chuckled and said
"I'm Johnny Strike."
It probably wasn't a miracle,
but I couldn't believe it.
Here was the guy who wrote
Crime's 1976 classic
"Hot Wire My Heart,"
which Sonic Youth covered
on their 1987 classic, *Sister*,
which I was listening to
on my Walkman
at the end of Mexico in the sun.
Except actually I was
listening to *Daydream Nation*,
I change it to *Sister*
when I tell that story.
But it's a beautiful story
even without embellishment.
That's another of the Oaxacan
experiences I mentioned,
but the rest are secrets.
Oh Mexico, as James Schuyler
wrote to Frank O'Hara,
are you just another
dissembling dream?
Schuyler was too tender
for me then, but now

he is just tender enough.
I love his wishes.
That "the beautiful humorous
white whippet" could
be immortal, for instance.
But I can't always forgive
his Central Park West tone,
his Austrian operettas
and long long lawns,
though he wasn't rich
and was tormented
enough, God knows.
In the summer of 1984
in Salida, Colorado,
I had Slade and Steve Perry
on my Walkman.
I drank milk from jumbo
Burger King glasses
emblazoned with scenes
from *Return of the Jedi*.
You can't buy tampons
with food stamps
even if your mother
insists that you try.
Salida sits along
the Arkansas River,
whose current
one hot afternoon
swept me away

and deposited me
in a shallow far downstream.
It was the first time
I thought I was going
to die and didn't. The Arkansas
and everything else are mortal.
My mom had been born again,
to my chagrin. But lately I find
I do believe in God
the Father Almighty, Maker
of heaven and earth:
and in Jesus Christ,
his Son our Lord,
who was conceived by
the Holy Ghost. How
the hell did I become
a Christian? Grace,
I guess. It just sort of
happened. I admit I find
the resurrection of the body
and life everlasting
difficult, or not difficult,
exactly, but impossible.
There is no crazier belief
than that we won't be
covered by leaves, leaves,
leaves, as Schuyler has it,
which is to say, really gone,
as O'Hara put it in his lovely

sad poem to John Ashbery.
But hope is a different animal
from belief. "The crazy hope
that Paul proclaims in 2
Corinthians," my friend John
wrote to me when his mother
died. The Christian religion
is very beautiful sometimes
and very true at other times,
though sophisticated persons
are still expected to be above
all that sort of thing. Well,
I'm a Marxist
too. Go and sell that thou
hast, and give to the poor.
On his new album Dr. Dre
says "Anybody complaining
about their circumstances
lost me." At the risk of losing
more billionaires, complain
about your circumstances,
I say. I listened to *The Chronic*
on my Walkman the summer
I worked the night shift
at Kinko's. I was dating Deirdre,
who when I placed my headphones
on her ears and pushed play
said "Why is this man cursing
at me?" Said it more loudly

than was strictly necessary.
A crazy man
would come into Kinko's
around two a.m. and ask me
to fax dire, scribbled warnings
to every news outlet in Denver.
He wanted to let people know
that God would punish the area
with natural disasters
if the county succeeded
in evicting him from the land
he was squatting on. He'd ask me
to help him think of various
extreme weather events
that God might unleash.
I'd say "Typhoons?"
though we were in Colorado.
He'd scribble typhoons.
Scraps of dirty paper absolutely
covered front and back with ominous,
angrily scrawled black characters:
ATTN. NBC NIGHTLY NEWS THERE WILL
BE FIRES TORNADOES TYPHOONS.
I would help him compose his screeds
then fax each one to Denver's
major TV and radio stations, the *Denver Post*,
and the *Rocky Mountain News*,
which has since stopped its presses
for good. Except in fact I would

only pretend to fax them
and then refuse his money,
saying I was glad to help the cause.
What if he wasn't batshit but a true
prophet? The Denver metropolitan area
was not visited by disaster
at that time, but this proves
nothing. Look at Jonah and
Nineveh, that great city.
I don't believe he was a prophet,
but Kinko's is beautiful
at two a.m. even if I hated
working there. The rows
of silent copiers
like retired dreadnoughts
in a back bay, the fluorescent
pallor, the classic-rock station
I would turn back up after
my coworker turned it down.
Did the guy sketch amateurish
floods, tornadoes, etc.,
on his jeremiads or did I
imagine that? I wish
I'd thought to make copies
for myself. I wish I'd kept
the Mexican girl's letter.
I wish I'd kept the copiers
with their slow arms
of light, the lights of DF

filling the Valley of Mexico
as the bus makes its slow way
down and Stevie sings what you
had, oh, what you lost. Schuyler
and his wishes! "I wish it was
1938 or '39 again." "I wish
I could take an engine apart
and reassemble it." "I wish I'd
brought my book of enlightening
literary essays." "I wish I could press
snowflakes in a book like flowers."
That last one's my favorite. I wish
I'd written it. I would often kick
for months until driven back to a bar
by fear or boredom or both. I saw
Tomorrow Never Dies—starring
Pierce Brosnan, the second-worst
James Bond—in Oaxaca and
came out wishing my life were
romantic and exciting and charmed
or at least that I had someone
to talk to. So I stopped at the first
bar I saw, and someone
talked to me. It's so sad and
perfect to be young and alone
in the Zócalo when the little lights
come up like fish surfacing
beneath the moon and you want
to grab the people walking by

and say who are you, are you
as afraid as I am. And you don't
know that twenty years later
you'll be writing this poem.
Well, now I'm being sentimental
and forgetting that in those days
I wrote the worst poems ever.
"I held a guitar and trembled
and would not sing" is an actual
line I wrote! The typhoon guy
could have written better poetry.
Today I want to write about
how it's been almost twenty years
since I owned a Walkman.
Just think: there was a song
that I didn't know
would be the last song
I would ever play on a Walkman.
I listened to it like it was just
any old song,
because it was.

The Deep Heart's Core

We must stop feeling things
in the deep heart's core.
That's where the lies live.

If you would see what's behind you,
close your eyes. Shut your mouth
if you want to send people to hell.

You have to *want* to go to hell. Deserve's
got nothing to do with it.
Yet hell has a waiting list.

Well, that's how dumb I am,
feeling my way to hell one
name at a time.

You Haven't Texted Since Saturday

You haven't texted
since Saturday,
when I read Keith Waldrop's
translation of *Les Fleurs du Mal*
on a bench by whatever
that tower is on the hill
in Fort Greene Park
until you walked up
late as always and I do
mean always
in your dad's army jacket
and said "Hi, buddy"
in a tone that told me
all I needed to know,
although protocol dictated
that you should sit next to me
and spell it out
and we should hold each other
and cry and then pretend
everything was fine, would
be fine, was someday
before the final
trumpet, before heat death,
zero point, big rip
sure to be absolutely
perfectly completely
probably fine. And
though it wasn't and
wouldn't be,

I walked you to the G
then rode the C
to Jay Street–MetroTech.
Just now I took a break from
this retrospect
to smoke one of the Camels
in the sky-blue box marked
IL FUMO UCCIDE
you brought me from Italy
and page through a book
on contemporary physics.
"Something must be
very wrong," it said,
and I agreed,
although it turned out
the author meant that "no theory
of physics should produce
infinities with impunity."
I'd point out that every theory
of the heart
produces infinities
with impunity
if I were the kind of jerk
who uses *the heart*
to mean the human
tendency to make
others suffer
just because we
hate to suffer

alone. I'm sorry
I brought a fitted sheet
to the beach. I'm sorry
I'm selfish and determined
to make the worst
of everything. I'm
sorry language is a ship
that goes down
while you're building it.
The Hesychasts of Byzantium
stripped their prayers
of words. It's been tried
with poems too. But insofar
as I am a disappointment
to myself and others, it seems fitting
to set up shop in almost
and not quite and that's not
what I meant. I draw the line at *the heart*,
though, with its
infinities. And I have to say
I am not a big fan
of being sad. Some people
can pull it off. When
we hiked Overlook, you
went on ahead to the summit
while I sat on a rock
reading Thomas Bernhard.
I'd just made it to the ruins
of the old hotel

when you came jogging back down
in your sports bra
saying I had to come see the view.
But my allergies were bad
and I was thirsty,
so we headed down the gravelly trail,
pleased by the occasional
advent of a jittery
chipmunk. You showed me pictures
on your phone of the fire
tower, the nineteenth-
century graffiti carved
into the rock, and the long
unfolded valley
of the Hudson. At the bottom,
the Buddhists let us
fill our water bottles
from their drinking fountain.
We called a cab and sat
along the roadside
watching prayer flags
rush in the wind. I said the wind
carried the prayers
inscribed on the flags
to the gods, but Wikipedia
informs me now that
> the Tibetans believe the prayers and mantras will be blown by the wind to spread
> good will and compassion into all pervading space.
So I was wrong, again,

about the gods. Wherever
you are, I hope you stand
still now and then
and let the prayers
wash over you like the breakers
at Fort Tilden that day
the huge gray gothic
clouds massed and threatened to drop
a storm on our heads
but didn't.

Shed

I wish I had a shed out back
of a house in an open
place and I'd sit in the cold
shed on quiet nights when all
the televisions go out and
the wires and the other wires
sing, and wonder what the small
things think about. A bitumen
boat in a royal tomb and a snake
and an angel too. Away from
loss prevention officers and
11 Secrets to Refinancing Your
Student Loans. I don't mean
some romantic Unabomber
shit, just a shed. The light
from a candle in the shed's
single window tosses a golden
square upon the snow that I
now see should surround
and shroud the shed. I hate
winter, so these snows must
be aesthetic. The December
before last I didn't leave my
apartment except for bodega
runs to stock up on Diet Coke
and peanut butter. I watched
every Anthony Mann Western
and spent half a day trying to
arrange Cheez-Its into the form

of Jimmy Stewart's face, then
ate the face. Some sorrow is
so baroque you look back
on it and feel like a schmuck.
Just yesterday the CBD Lifestyle
Station clerk asked how I was
and I said "Good, and you?" like
you're supposed to, like they teach
you in disaster simulations. I
know how to feel in my shed,
away from these statues
of assholes on horses,
and I let the shed field
the questions. Even in my
shed I want a shed.

When Didn't I Know It

I was born without language
and thus without the ability
to formulate a plan.
It was a few years after
the moon fell
to an American incursion.
I was smaller then
and prone to fits of pique.
I began to learn things
about dinosaurs and the way
a bag of vending-machine chips
will sometimes get stuck
on the Slinky-like contraption
that pushes it into free fall.
And there is no remedy;
according to the system
a fair transaction was concluded.
I learned that airplanes hang
on wires from ceilings.
I feared wasps. I remained
outside most churches.
I required stitches.
I was an expert on Bigfoot,
a reputed hominid
called *sásq'ets*
by the First Nations peoples.
I watched the moon
precisely blot the sun
on the wall of a shoebox.

As for Sea-Monkeys,
they did not, in fact, ride
one another like cowboys
on ponies or follow
a candle beam as if hypnotized.
Cobalt gives off—scientists
say "emits"—electrons. I
read that. I read about little
houses, big horses, assistant
pig-keepers, red ferns.
In those days of products
without clocks, I called
a number to hear
the time and temperature.
I blasted asteroids
into dust. I inflated tomatoes
with an air pump.
I flipped the dial
quickly back and forth
to glimpse
for a sublime instant
the Playboy Channel. I wanted
my MTV. And I strode.
I petted animals.
There was lots of dirt.
There were more trees then
and fewer on fire.
I trick-or-treated,

knowing little about stars,
less about cost.
In those days, when you lost
something, either you found it
or it stayed lost.

What They Mean

Less is more, they say. Lucky me.
Cicada reciting its lessons.
Rain smells like a VCR. Lizard moves
like a ring you try to
grab as it slips down the drain.

My sister sent me Klonopin
to help me savor shadows
on the cave wall. Requesting
immediate evac from the tarmac.

Jays raise a ruckus. Hit pause.
Press play. Gridlock, less
pay. Mask on? Wax off.
Mice's plans, they say,

go apeshit. They say
what you love will live on after.
What they mean is
here's a noose and there's a rafter.

CVS on Fire

The CVS on fire on Fox News
and the Fox News truck on fire
on Fox News and the quick
brown fox of the flames
jumping out of the frame are
one. And the night
advancing behind its riot
shield and the big small-town
moon bobble-head bobbing
outside Quicker Cash and
the late-shift Liquor Locker
clerk clocking the CVS
are one with the eternal rock-seated
being, the kingdom of one stone
upon another. I want to believe
there is a mammoth
in the ice of a flipside America
within whose filthy coat no bank
can find us. My kingdom
for a mammoth of heaven
and flame, a many-feathered
shaft-shouldered Fox News truck
invisible to the police. May earth
destroy CVS, may thistle
and sedge and dill and dock
wreck Fox. The yew is a hard tree,
fixed in the earth. The earth
is a hard earth. The grasslands
are wrapped in black wool.

The marshmallow charms and
palm-twigged paternoster
are yours. We'll follow the two stars
you can see from the city. This is
the five-ton day of the mastodon.
This has happened before. The
earth is hard and rain
is real and flint is cold. The flame
in the rag in the gas in the bottle
in the hand in the air in the future.

Bear

The internet mourned over the weekend after unconfirmed reports that Pedals, a bear that walked upright on its hind legs and was often captured on video strolling around New Jersey suburbs, may have been killed by a hunter.

—THE NEW YORK TIMES

They shot the bear that walked like a man;
they shot some bears that walked like bears.
I walk on as few legs as I can.
Don't shoot me if I put on airs.

Flare

I watch the range for signal fires.
I grow increasingly convinced
the message I've been waiting for
all my life will read: *wait*.
Burros in arroyos bray.
Hardly a day goes by.

Prayer

The path is for walking,
the tree is for shade.
God is for glory.
The day is for trade.

The path is for leaving,
the light for the west.
God is forgiving.
The dark is for rest.

I'm Talking to Trucks

I'm talking to trucks out here. I'm
getting closer. The power's
been out all day, the day draws
its power from other days.
The tree has a bear problem. *I*
would have shit my pants, you said
when I told you about the bears.
I'll never learn woody vines, nor
am I likely to follow anything
to its source. But I've been meaning
to tell you the red eft form
of the red-spotted newt remains
ashore for one to three years
then returns to the water
to change. Sometimes the land
stage is omitted. I'm in no hurry.
I'm talking to Wiedy's Furniture
Center. I put my clothes on, take
them off, talk to them. I read
aloud to my shoes, to whatever
the crystal you gave me's called.
I wish we could meet tomorrow
for the first time. The bastards
have installed lights everywhere
and they turn them on at night
as if the stars don't matter.
Everyone is insane. Not that,
as I said, the lights are on
at the moment. I'm running

on 37% battery power here.
News says it was above freezing
in the Arctic in February. So you
can't just oppose the everyday
as such to capital. I tell the bears
out there stay out there. Oh,
we're back: fridge hum, blinking
microwave, bright wings.
I lose my grip on things.
To get here, take the bus
that follows the roads that lead
to here. Sit on rock near water
beneath sun and leaf. Meet the new
moon, same as the old moon.
I explain to various industrial
solvents that the absence
of differential grave goods
suggests that early societies
were relatively egalitarian.
The Akkadian word for epidemic
disease meant *certain death*.
All death is certain, I guess.
Actually, tomorrow's no good
for me. I need to crouch
behind the church and wait
for the bear to reappear.
The church people are too polite
to ask what I'm doing. I haven't
talked to a human being in forever.

The humblest facts whisper to
the director of market research.
The land has a road in its side
and no one is free or easy.
Sometimes when I'm discussing
snowpack lows with Levon Helm
Memorial Boulevard, your name
comes up. Radiance and related
phenomena, past their sell-by date.
So I wait. I guess when you drop
something the lights let you see it
clearly enough to leave it where it falls.

Throwing the *Yijing* in Bullhead City

I pray the day
away, refuse
the news. So hot
your eyes bug out your skull.
I remember when these empties
were full. Sweet is the interstate
sighing above Desert Baptist.
There is only one prayer: Lord,
how do I get out
from under.
Thirsty sitter, at last,
sit fast, and thirst. The first
shall be last. And
the last shall be last. Two
Subarus is a coincidence,
four Subarus
is a sign. There are zero
yarrow sticks in this town
but I have two pennies and faith
that a third
may be procured.
Below the Mountain
emerges the Spring. Well,
that sure clears things up. I hate
titles like "Throwing the *Yijing* in
Bullhead City." "Feeding the Ducks
with Father Time." I hate how ghosts
take everything
so literally. There were few megafires

when I was a kid.
Now there's one on every block.
The desert's too hot
to burn. It just sits there
attracting mendicants
and holy hooey and very few
pennies. I was out there
38 days and nights,
nearly a record. But I'm OK,
I'm just dying. I'll be
OK in a minute.
I saw a billboard that said HELL IS REAL.
Well, duh,
they put up a billboard in it.

Poem

Scallop draggers far offshore
pull up tusks where long before
megafauna browsed in grass—
ocean now. This too shall pass.

County Fair

The jug band's on the gazebo, the swap meet
ends in profane oaths, a three-legged man
wins the three-legged race. Wiccans
stick horseshoe-shaped portals in the lawn
for croquet, which no one knows how to play.
Painted wood mallets thwock painted wood balls,
some wag yells *Fore!* and a ball's in the pond.
The winner and loser of the log-rolling contest
are in the same boat. There's room for
the plumber perched above the dunk tank.
A goldfish in its element in a baggie
will later go the way of all flush. The Sea
Dragon lifts from the turf at perihelion.
Kids petting goats get cryptosporidium.
Cotton candy rises to a cardboard cone.
Top 20 Country Countdown at the Cattle Call.
The log is more of a trunk, the dunk tank
more of a drunk tank, the Wiccans
a sticking point for the Jesus freak who,
like an old-time circus geek, is biting
someone's head off, and now
the hawser is dragged across
the mudhole for tug of war. Each side
is determined to stay upright and clean.

To Anthony Madrid

I act like I know it all. But you,
you act like you know it all.
We can't both be wrong. Still,
neither of us should have children.

Your head's in a sack. In a sack
with a snake with two heads.
And my head is even older than
our initial calculations implied.

I know many names for sitting cross-legged,
none for never getting up again.
You, you speak as if you just checked,
but it's not even up to you.

Fox pulls a rabbit out of a duck
and keeps the wound-up hounds upwind.
Hedgehog carries one trick around
like a small booth atop an elephant.

And both of us, elephant and booth,
carry from birth what can't be cast off
by dying. How can we corrupt the young?
The young don't even know we exist.

Past One O'Clock

I'll quit smoking
as soon as I
get lung cancer.
The young don't smoke
anymore, they join gyms.
I can't help thinking
they've misunderstood
something. The body's
a temple? The mind
is a tempest. Somewhere
along the line
the alternating stresses fall.
And if I quit smoking
how would I signal you?
The smoke alarm
pings me awake
to tell me it's dying.
OK! I will get up
to address again
the not-fire and maybe
all creation. I mean,
as long as I'm up.

Down the small
rain is the way
of things, my umbrella's
a dead spider,
so I pop
into the bodega and buy

one for $4
which turns out
to be impossible
to close once opened
which I mention
to the bodega guy
next time I pop in
who says yeah
that's why they're so cheap.
So I walk through
the rain's "pockmarked
face" to the apartment
where David Attenborough
emotionally manipulates
me re snow-leopard cub.
Everyone these days
feels like Werner Herzog
listening to
Timothy Treadwell's cries.

Past one o'clock.
I must have gone to bed.
I must have spent Christmas morning
reading the paper
in a gas-station diner in Lamar,
Colorado. Almost
one whole barn
beached by hay tides
a century ago.

It snows on crows.
And other pretty
observations. I said to Anthony,
regarding an older poet,
"He's always like,
The moon
has left her face
in the well." We both thought
that was rich.
The material social
order is a swindle,
cops kill kids,
and I'm writing
bourgeois shit
about prayer flags.
If you bring forth
what is within you,
the Gospel of Thomas
says, what you bring
forth will save you.
Within me, at last
inventory: student debt,
resentment, self-pity.
So here, I bring it forth,
you take it.

You must change your
etc. I have wasted
my etc. I dunno, maybe

sometimes God
intercedes by not
interceding so you lose
your faith and it's the loss
that saves you. Maybe
when I finally burn
the temple in the forest
within me and trash
the smoking effigy
of an old god reputed
to be strong
in many medicines—
maybe then I'll become
an eye, one among many,
borne by flatcars
to be conveyed via crane
and forklift to my destiny
upon the deep. To be all
eye and eye alone.

Yeah, well, good luck
with that. An earnest
young man with a clipboard
asks if I have a moment
for the environment. Uh,
what's it done for me lately?
I'm up, kid, I'm on my way
to church, perhaps to pray

that young people like you
(except for the clipboard)
might hear my message:
if you don't smoke, start
and don't stop. It's not
a world to get so
damn worked up
about leaving.

The Park Is Full of People

It took me an hour to travel
one hour into the future.
It's terrible here, Prince still dead
in purple raiment. The giant
inflatable stick-figure man
flaps above the Hyundai dealership.
The third nor'easter of the season
whams in. It's midnight all
afternoon. Let the snow bury
the snow. Snow says the radio
shows no sign of letting up.

Now I'm further in the future.
I arrived here by living. In what I view
as a personal affront, the park
is full of people. My eyes are pleather
cushions behind which
change has fallen. There's
a hawk up there but you can't
just go around keeping tabs
on every bird you see. Someone
misquoted "moon full on the lawn"
as "moon full *of* the lawn" and now
I long for airless orbiting prairies.

The inflatable man snaps.
The raiment's remains gently weep.
The prairies prick up their ears.
The future—or as I like to call it,

5:31 p.m.—is finally on.
The sparkle of parts in the park
is going, gone. I used to know
someone, if you can believe that.
I can't. I'm here. I'm still
walking through all this
inflatable mess. Dogs are rushing
in twilight toward or away
from their names. I can't see
where that hawk got to.

In Time of Plague

The seraph touches a live coal
to somebody's lips
but not mine. If the message is good,
the oracle's real. If it's bad, well,
it's all nonsense anyway.
In my early twenties I shoplifted
a copy of *The Gospel of Thomas*
from Barnes & Noble.
I sometimes wish God
weren't so subtle,
but you get what you pay for.
A friend tweeted today:
"If you see ppl shoplifting
right now, have their fucking
back." Me, I'm avoiding stores.
Outside for the first time
in weeks, an eagle's wingspan
between me and the enemy.
The most deserted spot
I can find is the lot
behind the dilapidated
Seventh-day Adventist school.
Kids shoot hoops in front;
out back, dozens of drab
birds study empty plastic
containers of cake frosting.
The school must be in use
in times that pass for normal—
healthy potted plants

sun on windowsills—
but it looks like it could
collapse any moment.
Like everything else. The church
connected to the school
is missing a few stained panes,
its base painted an incongruous
baby blue. A school bus lists
to starboard in weeds.
A woman holding a Swiffer
Sweeper at port arms nods
to me as she passes. I nod
back, trying to convey
"Quite the shitshow."
Home, I wash my red
hands raw again and check
for seraphim. I've had it
up to here with God.
Those hip youth pastors
with their acoustic guitars
have the right idea: reduce
it to bromides, sing-alongs,
manga Jesus. Whatever
survives that must be true.
Hey, did I ever tell you about
the time I prayed for help
and help came there none?
It was a day much like this one.
It's dark inside God at first.

You gotta make your own
spark, like those red lamps
on the ocean floor
that illuminate their prey
right before they attack.

John Says the Elders Came Over

John says the elders came over
to let him know the dome
light in his car was on.
I assume he turned it off.
I called Mark and most
of our sentences began
Do you remember the night . . .
Angie said—posted,
rather—her cat died.
Cat she got the Fourth
of July '95
when we broke the sink
in the bathroom at Kirby's.
Leigha said she was there
too, and that's right, she was.
A lot can happen
on the Fourth in Wichita.
Kids cruise Circle K,
toss Black Cats, dance away.
They told me I'd get
over it. I did. They said
it's not the end of the world.
It was. Big fireworks
above the wide river, like
a music video, like
a prayer. Someone gets filled
with the Spirit, someone else
says they don't want to hear it.
Jerry has a month to live,

but I will get by. I'm like you.
Got my game face on.
I'm a backup genny
kicking in. No, wait, that's
someone else. I'm
basic. Like Wichita, birthplace
of Pizza Hut, where I grew up
between Weatherman and
Walkman. I am
pretty solidly here, Kirby's
is still there, our dead
pets and Jerry are
probably nowhere. Wichita,
my rear-view mirror,
turning and turning
in the tornado sutra,
let's not meet again.
It's a good century
for staying in.

The Seasons

The star that looks awry upon the sinner
orients the temple. Mother Kate places
the wafer in my hands, a story
about a body. I read insects
worldwide are facing Krefeld-level
declines. Krefeld is in Germany, I
read. Its insects declined. Tigers
and polar bears get all the press.
In high school I jumped the barrier
at Cheyenne Mountain Zoo to reach
through the bars to pet a panther. He
was sleeping and woke with a small growl
of surprise. I hadn't read Rilke. Now,
I wouldn't want to bother a panther.
Let them out, let them eat people.
Which brings us back to the Eucharist.
A fly alit upon the wafer, is my point.
It was a small part of the pantomime.
A spider spies the fly
with David Hedison's head
just before the rock
squashes them.
The consubstantiation
of Jeff Goldblum
in Cronenberg's remake
is slicker. I thought,
in my childhood,
as a child. I got lost in this
hypostasis. If there's one thing I know

I can't think of it at the moment.
Wait, I know Gram Parsons's friends
stole his body after his overdose
by posing as morticians
at LAX. They were so nervous
they drove the hearse
they'd borrowed from Gram's
assistant's girlfriend—
it was the '70s—
into the side of a hangar
right in front of a cop. But
the cop waved them on—it
was the '70s—and they lit out
for Joshua Tree, where they doused
Gram in gas and sparked a Bic.
My friends would blow
the heist somehow
but if I ever die,
and I probably will,
I want to be propped
against a dumpster
in Phoenicia, New York,
for bears to eat. Not slathered
in DEET for once. The black-legged
tick sure ain't in decline. Well,
it's not an insect. I hate
very few of nature's people.
That tick's at the top of the list.
The weedy species survive.

I like deer OK, but if you've seen
a trillion, you've seen 'em all.
Men shot all the wolves
so there's more deer
so there's more ticks.
I think I could shoot a man
who'd shoot a wolf.
I read this piece about
fascism and ecocide
that was like, "Despair
is not an option." Fuck
you: I've opted for it. Yeah,
I hope we rise like lions, live
every day like it's
Bastille Day. But men
shot all the lions. I used to shoot
cans and signs in the woods with Jay,
hippie hunter high on *duende*.
The fascists shot Lorca
against a dumpster
at LAX. Writing
home from New York
Lorca calls Protestantism
"the most ridiculous,
most odious thing in the world."
And Frank O'Hara's Lorca
adores "our tantrum of belief,"
which isn't in Lorca
but also sort of is.

We could do with a few
more tantrums, it's true.
I've sat through sermons
about *New Yorker* cartoons.
The Orthodox didn't make
Augustine's mistake
about original sin.
For Marx the shebang
begins with theft.
What thou lovest well
shall be reft. I forgot to take
my antidepressant last night
so I don't remember what
I meant to write next, but
as long as we're on the subject
I note that some scholars
discern a direct line
from the Protestant ethic
to the enclosure of commons.
The forests were "the nursery
and resort of the most idle
and profligate of men: here
the undergraduates in iniquity
commence their career
with deer stealing, and here
the more finished
and hardened robber
secrets himself from justice."
Deed land to the richest

sons of bitches for the moral
improvement of the poor.
I'm all for a little deer
stealing around Phoenicia.
Cioran says losing love
makes a hairdresser into
a rival of Socrates. Not that
this is about love—or losing
love, which amounts
to the same thing.
Phoenicia made me think
of bears, and bears led to
Romania—I read Ceaușescu
shot 400 bears—which led
to Cioran. In Phoenicia
I rivaled Socrates. This
isn't about that. Despair,
though, black-legged,
Krefeld-level, sure, what isn't
these days. A bald
eagle carries a kill
across a creek. I point my
phone at it but where it is
is too swiftly where
it used to be. That bear
two summers ago—
like seeing a refrigerator
sprint. All the forest's
pots and pans

clanging. Some days I still
believe God is whatever
God is. Mostly I fear the fools
are right. Doubt's part of the game,
says Mother Kate. The pasture
assembles a coyote
out of whatever it has
lying around, he is the color
of the tall rushes with a pretty
name I can barely tell
him apart from. I make him
nervous, I call "It's OK"
to where I think he is.
And I could swim
through the Lyme
vectors to the coyote,
but I don't need
to be forgiven. George Herbert
says somewhere
something useless. And with that
I reenter winter, wafer
thin as a story
about the body,
New York February
rock-salt-slush scuzz
a deli cat picks
her way across,
first the right
forefoot

carefully
then the etc. I went
a little Bible-crazy,
turning to a random page
to get a message from HR.
You can make anything
mean anything if you
press down hard enough.
Plastromancy, divination
by tortoise shell—heat
the shell with pokers,
interpret the resulting
cracks. Changes. Which
brings us back to Marx's
letters of blood
and fire. Climate crash,
dispossession of commons
writ global, Shell spill
crackling in flame, minus
divinity. The trinity—
capital, land, labor—
falls apart. The auction
cannot hear the auctioneer.
I read moose are dying
of tick infestation—a hundred
thousand ticks on a single
cow. I read monarch
flight paths are disappearing.
I read this terrible thing is

causing that terrible thing.
I read you don't know
what you got till it's gone.
I read something bad
is happening to glaciers. I read
something bad is happening
to coral. I read something
bad is happening to frogs.
I read that I have disaster
fatigue. I searched *how to*
fight disaster fatigue.
I searched *A2 emissions*
scenario. I searched *Standing*
Rock Sunoco, garbage
fire, I searched *holy*
forking shirtballs. I read clouds
are endangered—fucking
clouds. I read again
and again humans are
responsible. Nah. *Some*
humans are responsible.
How many oil refineries
does your average goatherd
own? Last summer
California burned, like
the autumn before and
the summer before and
the autumn before that.
Used to be if you wrote

about trees and clouds
you were a *nature poet*,
floating mistily
above the social. Now
not to speak of trees
is almost a crime.
As for bees,
the revery alone will
have to do. Swim out
past the breakers, watch
the woods fill up
with fire. OK, I'll
stop. This species, that
ice shelf—we get it,
we're fucked. The raccoon
came and curled up
on the porch every time
I went out to smoke
for a week. Each of us
minding his own business
so as not to scare
the other off. Birds
do bird stuff. I don't know
what kind—small, brown, won't
shut up. The weathered house
on the ridge is human.
Not an Aries in sight, just
me and aforementioned
critters. I guess one of them

could be an Aries. I remember
how mad I got when the Aries
this isn't about nonchalantly
replied "Yeah, Mercury's
in retrograde" during an
argument. As if our crossed
wires and shitty feelings
were down to whatever
the hell that means. This guy
explained it to me, rising
signs and seventh houses
and all that, but I wasn't really
paying attention. He
also correctly guessed
my sign within two minutes
of meeting me. An 8%
chance. But the stars, man,
are not the goddamn
lonely ones in this
equation. You can't step twice
into the same summer
in West Kill, every sign
in the right house,
every house a home.
An entire basketball
season's come and gone,
all bad luck and injuries,
the streak of titles
snapped, an early

exit from the tourney.
This time last year
Devonte' Graham
was leading Kansas
to an improbable
Final Four. In hoops
there's always next
season—one reason
I prefer watching
basketball to rivaling
Socrates. I read that
thousands of bright
orange novelty phones
shaped like Garfield
have been washing up
on the Brittany shore
for thirty years. Pick up
the receiver and Garfield's
eyes slide half open.
My eyes slide half
closed as I read
about work bells
in the cloth-producing
towns of the fourteenth
century. Time was better before
it was space. Garfield sails
ringing in on the tide. I pick up.
The plastic bag on the floor
of the Challenger Deep

clears its throat and croons
into its matching Garfield: *Operator,*
could you help me place this call?
How could I answer the plastic bag
sliding half empty
across the floors of silent seas?
Seas are noisy now, though,
I read. I said I'd stop.
Don't tell me what I said.
I've never been to France—well,
I took a train across a sliver
of it one night, window
of French moon in French trees—
but I want to see that cave
where 35,000 years ago
people whose brains
were larger than ours
by a single tennis ball
realized that the lines of aurochs
and wooly rhinoceros
might be preserved in charcoal
and hematite. Eye to hand,
wick in animal fat in stone bowl,
an impulse leading
to MoMA totes. Chauvet
is closed to the public,
of which I confess myself
a reluctant member. After
a good dog named Robot

discovered the Lascaux paintings,
visitors damaged the art
by breathing. So the French
government constructed a
life-sized replica of Chauvet
three miles away
"within a football-field-sized
cave made from a metal
scaffolding over a rock-
colored mortar." Even the smell
of the original cave
is duplicated. A metaphor
for—well, everything. To see
that early in that early
light. Art historians debate
whether the cave bears
and horses and ibex are
pictures in our sense. I pause
the documentary to study
the aurochs who looks
like Eeyore. John Berger
says art's an imitation
of creation not nature.
They let him into Chauvet,
the big shot. He died
the other day. I began this
in winter and now it's spring.
The cave paintings are Cro-Magnon
movies: the artist used contours

of rock and shadow
so by the quiver of torchlight
the animals gallop and flow.
No place that doesn't see you.
Spring so I go to the park,
everything greener
than real life. Half-naked
people with Frisbees
and plastic water bottles.
Dogs and phones far and wide.
I too have known the pleasure
of simple ritual: chasing
an orange ball, fetching it
in my mouth to drop
at a loved one's feet. I
stopped by St. Ann's yesterday,
Mother Kate said "Weird,
I was just thinking of you."
I'd avoided church for months.
We talked as a strain of mild
EDM drifted through a window.
In the park a guitar-violin duo
plays the *Game of Thrones* theme
then "Come On Eileen"
and "The Tide Is High"
then tries my goodwill with Leonard Cohen.
I sit on a railing near the men's room
and they slide into a good song
people think is a bad song.

It's sad and it's sweet
and I knew it complete
when I wore a younger man's clothes.
Kate and I walked to the nave
across the balcony from which
the pews always make me think
of Scrabble. It rains
in the park and stops raining.
I put a dollar in the guitar case,
pet someone's whippet, head
to the angel to see the turtles.
Bumblebees big as baby
carrots bob on bluebells.
Are pretty observations
almost a crime? I told Kate
I have FOMO and everything's
being murdered. She gave me
a pamplemousse LaCroix.
The park in spring's in summer.
Seasons still signify, mostly.
The last aurochs died ten years
after Shakespeare. So what?
I asked Anthony who the most
pessimistic poet is, he said
"Maybe try Leopardi." I opened
Leopardi at random to "all human
hope is vain." The woman
at the information kiosk tries
to disseminate information

to me but I'm onto her.
Then I'm out of the park
into maximal blare.
It's always the end of the world
somewhere. Things gear up,
wind down. There's the Dakota,
John Lennon done in. I was in
Manitou Springs with *Sgt. Pepper's*
on 8-track. Yoko still lives there.

ACKNOWLEDGMENTS

Thanks to the editors of journals in which some of these poems first appeared: *Harvard Review, The Nation, The Paris Review, Poetry, The Sewanee Review.*

"Walkman" was published in *The Best American Poetry 2018.*

Super intense thanks to Anthony Madrid for setting the poems in this book in order when I was sick of looking at 'em, and for serving as a one-man workshop. *Je peux commencer une chose . . .*

Thanks as ever to Paige Ackerson-Kiely, Julia Kardon, Xa Robbins, and Paul Slovak.

Thanks to the Rev. Katherine Salisbury.

Thanks to Benjamin Kunkel for letting me steal something he said to me on the phone for the last sentence of "John Says the Elders Came Over."

The first line of "The Seasons" is lifted from a sermon by Jeremy Taylor. Other borrowings should be obvious.

Thanks to the Kansas Jayhawks men's basketball team, 2020 NCAA National Champions.

Thanks also to Carly Rae Jepsen, Blood Incantation, Eric Church, Rihanna, Opeth, Kacey Musgraves, Future, Converge, Miranda Lambert, Billie Eilish, Tomb Mold, the New Pornographers, Iron Maiden, Robyn, Power Trip, Bryan Ferry, Run the Jewels, Horrendous, Taylor Swift, Sweven, and Counting Crows.

And to John Prine, who I hope is now a poster of an old rodeo.

Michael Robbins now lives in New Jersey. He is the author of two previous poetry collections, *Alien vs. Predator* and *The Second Sex*, and *Equipment for Living: On Poetry and Pop Music*, a volume of essays, as well as the editor of *Margaret Cavendish*, a selection of the duchess's poems. He is an associate professor of English at Montclair State University.

GAROUS ABDOLMALEKIAN
*Lean Against This
   Late Hour*

PAIGE ACKERSON-
KIELY
Dolefully, A Rampart Stands

JOHN ASHBERY
Selected Poems
*Self-Portrait in a
   Convex Mirror*

PAUL BEATTY
Joker, Joker, Deuce

JOSHUA BENNETT
Owed
The Sobbing School

TED BERRIGAN
The Sonnets

LAUREN BERRY
The Lifting Dress

JOE BONOMO
Installations

PHILIP BOOTH
*Lifelines:
   Selected Poems
   1950–1999*
Selves

JIM CARROLL
*Fear of Dreaming:
   The Selected Poems*
Living at the Movies
Void of Course

ALISON HAWTHORNE
DEMING
Genius Loci
Rope
Stairway to Heaven

CARL DENNIS
Another Reason
Callings
*New and Selected Poems
   1974–2004*
Night School
Practical Gods
Ranking the Wishes
Unknown Friends

DIANE DI PRIMA
Loba

STUART DISCHELL
Backwards Days
Dig Safe

STEPHEN DOBYNS
*Velocities:
   New and Selected Poems:
   1966–1992*

EDWARD DORN
Way More West

HEID E. ERDRICH
Little Big Bully

ROGER FANNING
The Middle Ages

ADAM FOULDS
*The Broken Word:
   An Epic Poem of the
   British Empire in Kenya,
   and the Mau Mau Uprising
   Against It*

CARRIE FOUNTAIN
Burn Lake
Instant Winner
The Life

AMY GERSTLER
Dearest Creature
Ghost Girl
Index of Women
Medicine
Nerve Storm
Scattered at Sea

EUGENE GLORIA
*Drivers at the Short-Time
   Motel*
Hoodlum Birds
My Favorite Warlord
Sightseer in This Killing City

DEBORA GREGER
By Herself
*Desert Fathers,
   Uranium Daughters*
God
In Darwin's Room
Men, Women, and Ghosts
Western Art

TERRANCE HAYES
*American Sonnets for My
   Past and Future Assassin*
Hip Logic
How to Be Drawn
Lighthead
Wind in a Box

NATHAN HOKS
The Narrow Circle

ROBERT HUNTER
Sentinel and Other Poems

MARY KARR
Viper Rum

WILLIAM KECKLER
Sanskrit of the Body

JACK KEROUAC
Book of Blues
Book of Haikus
Book of Sketches

JOANNA KLINK
Circadian
*Excerpts from a Secret
   Prophecy*
The Nightfields
Raptus

JOANNE KYGER
*As Ever:
   Selected Poems*

ANN LAUTERBACH
Hum
*If in Time: Selected Poems,
   1975–2000*
On a Stair
Or to Begin Again
Spell
Under the Sign

CORINNE LEE
Plenty
Pyx

PHILLIS LEVIN
May Day
Mercury
Mr. Memory & Other Poems

PATRICIA LOCKWOOD
*Motherland Fatherland
   Homelandsexuals*

WILLIAM LOGAN
Macbeth in Venice
Madame X
Rift of Light
Strange Flesh
The Whispering Gallery

J. MICHAEL MARTINEZ
Museum of the Americas

ADRIAN MATEJKA
The Big Smoke
Map to the Stars
Mixology
Somebody Else Sold the
  World

MICHAEL MCCLURE
Huge Dreams:
  San Francisco and
  Beat Poems

ROSE MCLARNEY
Forage
Its Day Being Gone

DAVID MELTZER
David's Copy:
  The Selected Poems
  of David Meltzer

ROBERT MORGAN
Dark Energy
Terroir

CAROL MUSKE-DUKES
Blue Rose
An Octave Above Thunder:
  New and Selected Poems
Red Trousseau
Twin Cities

ALICE NOTLEY
Certain Magical Acts
Culture of One
The Descent of Alette
Disobedience
For the Ride
In the Pines
Mysteries of Small Houses

WILLIE PERDOMO
The Crazy Bunch
The Essential Hits of
  Shorty Bon Bon

DANIEL POPPICK
Fear of Description

LIA PURPURA
It Shouldn't Have Been
  Beautiful

LAWRENCE RAAB
The History of Forgetting
Visible Signs:
  New and Selected Poems

BARBARA RAS
The Last Skin
One Hidden Stuff

MICHAEL ROBBINS
Alien vs. Predator
The Second Sex
Walkman

PATTIANN ROGERS
Generations
Holy Heathen Rhapsody
Quickening Fields
Wayfare

SAM SAX
Madness

ROBYN SCHIFF
A Woman of Property

WILLIAM STOBB
Absentia
Nervous Systems

TRYFON TOLIDES
An Almost Pure Empty
  Walking

VINCENT TORO
Tertulia

SARAH VAP
Viability

ANNE WALDMAN
Gossamurmur
Kill or Cure
Manatee/Humanity
Trickster Feminism

JAMES WELCH
Riding the Earthboy 40

PHILIP WHALEN
Overtime: Selected Poems

ROBERT WRIGLEY
Anatomy of Melancholy and
  Other Poems
Beautiful Country
Box
Earthly Meditations:
  New and Selected Poems
Lives of the Animals
Reign of Snakes

MARK YAKICH
The Importance of Peeling
  Potatoes in Ukraine
Spiritual Exercises
Unrelated Individuals
  Forming a Group Waiting
  to Cross